Rohinton Daruwala lives and works in Pune, India. He writes code for a living, and poetry and speculative fiction when he can. He tweets as @wordbandar and blogs at wordbandar.wordpress.com. His work has previously appeared in the anthology *To Catch a Poem* and in magazines such as *Strange Horizons, New Myths, Star*Line, Liminality* and *Through the Gate*.

the sand libraries of timbuktu

~poems~

Rohinton Daruwala

SPEAKING TIGER

In association with the Jehangir Sabavala Foundation

To Jhumur and Sudarshan

SPEAKING TIGER PUBLISHING PVT. LTD
4381/4, Ansari Road, Daryaganj,
New Delhi–110002, India

First published in India by Speaking Tiger in hardback 2016

ISBN: 978-93-86050-05-2
eISBN: 978-93-86050-07-6

10 9 8 7 6 5 4 3 2 1

Typeset in Requiem Regular by SÜRYA, New Delhi
Printed at Sanat Printers, Kundli.

Contents

Tea, Coffee and Cigarettes

Morning Tea Meditation

Brewed long, brewed warm,
in the civilized patience of pure porcelain,
poured out like a household blessing.
Hands clasped round the cup, meditate
on the self-satisfied teapot,
growing brown liquid contentment within itself.
Sip long and slow at this cup,
wash yourself over with its contentment,
and learn the wisdom of sitting still.

Making Tea

Boil the water, she says,
till it's warmer than common lust,
but cooler than a hot temper.

Pour the water, let it sit
longer than an impatient child's pleading,
but not as long as brooding jealousy.

Pour it out into cups.
Add sugar sweeter than kindness,
but not as saccharine as indulgence.

Stir after you add milk,
enough for the colour of compassion,
but not for the shade of weakness.

Serve it with courtesy
that falls short of servitude,
and sip it slowly, with gratitude.

Single Seating

He's seated on a chair
at a desk facing the wall.
Clink of teacup.
Click of mouse.

Turned away from all the other
Coffee-shop tables, his broad shoulders
hide his laptop screen well
with just the screen flicker on his glasses
and the peppermint wafting over from
his teacup to indicate life.
Clink of teacup.
Click of mouse.

Pairwise tables ringed around him,
He's a star finishing his makeup;
an actor turning away
to weep dramatically;
a troll hiding under the
mini-staircase to the mezzanine floor.
Clink of teacup.
Click of mouse.

A waiter slips in cups between
flirtations of varying finesse;
crowbars the bill in between
a heated argument and artfully
ignores three other tables.
But through it all, typing and typing,
the man is oblivious.
Clink of teacup.
Click of mouse.

He is so rooted, I sip and watch
him with a clink of my teacup,
his shoulders showing the barest
vibration of typing, then stopping for
a click of mouse.

I imagine one of him in
every building I've ever seen,
an unregarded pillar,
a shy retiring gargoyle,
and in my distracted mind
he seems so absolutely essential
until,
I notice his empty chair.
Clink of teacup.

Cigarettes and Dawn

His old-man fingers shake a little
as he lights up the unfinished morning
and speaks—

'The myths are all wrong.
Prometheus as a clumsy,
found-out thief.
The real discoverers of fire
were a couple of Neanderthals
trying to light up a joint.'

He takes another puff
after the joke's spilled out of him like smoke.
A sliver of ash
falls onto the table like grey rain.

'Ask yourself just what I'm smoking,'
he says,
'You'll probably start
with the smoke rings
'cause they're so pretty,
and that's as good a reason as anything.
I'll bet you could float up there
for years and years.

'Then, later,
you might get down
and double up on the ash,
evidence of the crime,
and maybe you're real smart with evidence.
You'll have at it with cold science
and all your machines of logic.

'And, later still,
you'll think about the cigarette itself.
You'll get past brand names,
sink those fingers
right into the tobacco, the paper.
You'll smoke 'em yourself,
the real, real experience,
and then you'll think
you've got me.'

He coughs, and then
his voice lies still on the silence
as if it were rich carpeting.

'If you're lucky,'
he says,
'you'll catch a glimpse of the flame,
and maybe you'll get
to stare at it a little,
baby-eyed unblinking,
before it goes out.'

He's done smoking, and as he gets up
to walk into a pink-grey morning
of half-filled tea glasses,
he's got an old man's face,
craggy and unshaven
with yellowed teeth
and two unblinking coal-black eyes
that could stare the sun into shame.

Love Poems

SMS Poem

Stray hair on a pillow,
a teacup,
a slice of toast,
three open books,
a Post-it,
seven messages
and five emails.
The joy of a day spent collecting you.

Seduction by Fruit

Drunk, on your cider-sweet breath,
I devour the scent of apples,
clinging madly to the last bite.
She shakes her head in disappointment.

Plucking the raisin tips
of your ripe mango breasts.
Stop, she says, before I
have to get up and leave.

Picked up each of your angry words,
peeled them like litchis,
to expose the sweetness within.
Nice, she says, but not enough.

String you out into six hundred
soft gasps of pleasure,
swallowed whole or peeled like
quivering grapes between my teeth.

She says nothing,
takes three perfect grapes,
and crushes them
between her irresistible teeth.

She smiles and waits with
a knowing patience for
me to kiss the drop
of juice beside her lips.

Diwali

You're up early
while I'm still sleeping.
You have a puja to perform
of course.

So many names
for you to remember
of so many relatives crowding in.
I'm sure

You've forgotten
my name that lies afloat
like oil on a diya lit late
last night.

You're dressed
in a bright, bright sari
that you're happily uncomfortable
wearing.

And unseemly
I am more concerned with
the taking off than the putting
on of it.

Past evening
I will walk to you through
the sulphur of exploded
crackers

and stop
your mouth for a kiss with
your body soft between
my arms

like a broken-off piece of mithai.

Ugli Fruit

Would you be green
if I picked a tangerine?

Would you be yellow
if you caught me with a pomelo?

Would you care to kiss the nape
of the neck of a grape?

Or would you prefer to grapple with an apple?

Or dawdle and sample
a chickoo or two?

Another week till spring
drops off into rot.

Remember, some day
they'll all taste the same,
and that some fruits
are ugly only in name.

Upside-down Kiss

Upper lip on lower lip,
lower lip on upper,
held together delicately,
before they part into each other.

My nose fits cutely
into your dimpled chin,
your breath on my neck
stumbles like a startled mare.

You on a sofa, me behind,
tipping your head back
with my fingers,
or you flat on a bed.

My eyes hold yours,
while my face descends,
clumsy until my tongue finds
the warm familiarity of yours.

Mouth raised, my gaze tumbles
down your lovely neck and breasts.
My eyes read yours, I search
for a sign of amusement.

But they only say to me—
so this is technique then,
turning the same body upside down
on the same familiar sheets.

Your Name

It comes to me with a soft
shock of pleasure, finding
your name in print or
in speech.

Surely your name does not
embody you. You cannot
be spelled out in a
few letters.

Yet, there are times,
interrupted in thought,
your name tumbles out of
my mouth

like a flower held
between my fingers
that drops softly to
the floor.

Later on, of course
there will be other names,
sweeter, more intimate and
unshared.

But until then, this name,
with its worn unfamiliar
petals, this name of yours,
will do.

Rain Poems

Rain Gathering

This morning when it rained,
I made up my mind
to gather all of the rain
and hoard every single drop.

I went outside, and as
soon as the first drops
began to fall, I stretched out
my hands and tried to gather them all.

But the drops escaped me.
I tilted open my mouth,
and tried to swallow them, but I
choked and spluttered myself into embarrassment.

Sitting here, far away now,
I know well enough not
to try cheap bottles and vessels
and anyway, stale water is useless to me.

I now know to sit still
and gather only the sound
some raindrops make, feel them
through the pores of my being,
grateful for the stain each one leaves.

The Rain Outside

I spent all day missing the rain
hugging myself indoors.
It danced outside my window pane,
silenced through concrete floors.

I ran my hands over
comfortably untouched skin,
wrapped myself in silence.
Outside, the tumult and the din.

Before it started, I watched
the wind torment the trees,
run its dusty feet through the streets,
and slowly cause the darkness to increase.

I find clouds of work
to bury myself in, and listen
only to the soothing pitter-patter
of the next task's distraction.

But I cannot help turning
to the restless dancing trees.
My untouched skin begins to imagine
the touch of the wind and the breeze.

I cannot keep still.
The storm without calls the storm within,
and my restless body longs
to join the tumult and the din.

In the end I can bear no more.
My body feels the end of its wait
I rise and stumble to the door,
but it is already too late.

In the end my uncertain mind
has taken too long to decide.
I try the door only to find
that I've locked myself inside.

Memories of Water

Alone, on a parched day I
wander silent empty rooms,
my dry soles beating out a
rhythm of distant liquid longings.
I put myself under a bathroom shower,
and in my private rainstorm
watch cold jewels slip down my
skin and shatter noiselessly.
I drink in the shower water.
I cannot get enough.
I suck dry taps, bottles, ice cubes,
freezer frost till I threaten to burst.
And then I lie silent
on the cold tiled floor, and
the liquid inside me dreams. I
am a cold floating ocean of dreams.
And the water dreams of sunlight
like sweet music, that kisses it
with the honey lips of morning,
as gentle as the dawn.

It dreams of days when it
wrapped itself in a cloak of sky
and ran past rocks, singing
brightly into their hard ears.
And it dreams also of darknesses,
of running through rocky caverns,
and lying ever so still in
forgotten silent pools like grey mirrors.

The water dreams of men also.
Inside of me, it slop slop slops
against the inside of my skull,
dissolving memories into itself.

I saw a man being beaten once.
They whipped him with leather belts
and curses, and I watched
with a crowd of useless impotents.
It was a murky grey-skied day,
the kind that hatred breeds. Either
the man would bleed or it would rain.
Red drops fell when clear ones didn't.
I do not know if he died there.
I do not know if he lived afterwards.
I do not know if he sobbed and sobbed
in shame as I was never able to.

On the floor I turn over and over,
until the tears come in a tide.
I lie face down, palms down,
lips touching the salt-wet tiles.
I get up and shower again.
I watch the water run into
the drain dragging skin and hair
with it and I realize something.

Water remembers, but it cannot see.
It accepts, it absorbs, it swallows
what comes to it without question
or comment. It cannot be sated.
It lies still on wet floors,
in closed taps, on kitchen counters,
in glasses, in bottles, in the air
we breathe in and out, in our bodies.
It hears me sleeping and waking, talking
and listening, alone and embraced.
It hears me make love to my wife and
to myself. It hears me laughing.
And yet it cannot know what a man
is. What a woman is. It
cannot count the million lovely breaths
that flow in and out of a breast.
It carries only shadows in itself,
flat mirror images of feeling.
And yet the sea is endless. The sea
holds worlds and worlds within itself.

And I feel the substance of myself
drawn slowly to the sea,
down the long fingers of time,
breath by whispering breath.

Rain Poem

I

‘Good news my darling, it rained today,’
I announce loudly, tumbling
droplets onto a white-tiled floor.
‘I’ve been walking, wading
through so many fresh rivulets.
It took the rain an hour
to wash off so many months of sweat.
My lungs were breathing cool air
all along the way here. I’ve been
hearing a rolling tumbling music
and been bathed in drunken laughter.’

Peeling out of my wet clothes I say,
‘Ten streets and only one umbrella.
The rest of us washing our hair,
and this bald fellow stoutly dry,
tone deaf to the rain.’
Amused, she watches me undress
and says,
‘With all that music, you could’ve
given me a more graceful striptease.’

As I shower, she talks to me
through a closed door, her words
dripping onto the floor and pulling out
strange patterns from water and street dirt.
'The lights were out while you were gone,'
she says, 'it nearly drowned me,
drew me up in a soft, warm black bag,
left me screaming in dark, black ink.
I could hear the rain all around me
and the darkness all through the city.
I could see you walking in the darkness,
and stumbling and falling and not getting up.
I stood over you and watched you die,
drowned you in my own salt tears.
You saw my face framed in lightning,
like an unhappy ghost saying goodbye.'

'And then the lights came on,' I say,
opening the door a little. 'No,' she says,
handing me the forgotten towel,
'I just learned how to see in the dark.'

II

She's cold when I hold her,
and her lips speak to me
of the storm in waiting,
of the tempest sleeping in skin.
Lightning carves up the sky.
The earth resists the raindrops,
tearing at its skin and then
melts into an explosion of fragrance.
I breathe it in along with
the sweat on her neck. We lie
skin wrapped in skin,
drowning in a mingled breath.
Her thigh resting against mine
moves an inch and disturbs the
soft sheets that wrap the
diffused warmth of our bodies.
Her breath washes past my ear
in ebbing tides. The perfume
from the dark forest of her hair
whispers to me in soft voices.
And then there is silence wrapped
in the drumming rhythm of rainwater.
She whispers to me that
the lights have gone off again.
I tell her I switched them off
before we started. And then,
there is only the silence
wrapped in rain-soaked skin.

Her ears are sharper than mine.
The light catches the earring
on a soft lobe, as it turns
to notice the dull sounds
of a leaking window.
There's a soft pool at the side of our bed.
In this darkness, I cannot tell
if it's warm blood or clear crystal,
as it's shattered by a new droplet.
And we talk, in her voice and mine,
in the mingled voices of the rain,
and the pool grows larger, its surface
pulsing between dream and nightmare.

She draws apart long enough
to gather sheets around us.
She hears the hollow beast sounds of the wind
and wraps us in a cloak of warmness.
And we drown together in sleep,
which is a final drowning,
drawn apart at last,
as rainwater slips between skin and skin.

III

The morning cheerily awakens me,
with fists of careless brightness,
determined to massage a healthy glow
onto poor rain-soaked skin.
The day, rid of the rain,
wraps itself in the ritual
of habit. Last night evaporates
in today's golden warmth.
I sit on a large, soft armchair,
drinking a comforting cup of tea,
trying to discern in the sunlight
shapes of burnt up dreams and nightmares.

She sings while she puts on
a second cup. Bright spirits
on a bright day, with neither
space nor time for senseless dreaming.

But there's hope yet. She curses
the dangerous storm-soaked days
and praises bright ones, but still
has left that window carefully unfixed.

The Woman in Flat 17

The city is dry, the city is hot.
The hundreds and hundreds unhappy with their lot,
use one arm to shield their dry paper faces
and with the other put their life through its paces.

The rain is late, the rain has failed.
The people have worried, rallied and emailed
their problems to all the right places,
heard empty promises, seen blank faces,

and now occupy themselves with idle gossip.

On this boiling, melting-hot day,
a careless step might lead you astray.
Where have you been to, have you been
talking to the woman in flat 17?

They say she moved in last week.
No one's been in, not even for a peek.
Have you seen her, have you seen
the mysterious woman in flat 17?

Mrs Sharma is sure she has never
seen a sari worn like that ever.
Surely there must be something obscene
about the woman in flat 17?

Visitors come after dark, leave before dawn,
never in cars, perhaps on foot or horse or even airborne?
It all sounds so unsavoury and unclean,
everything about the woman in flat 17.

One morning she's up on the building roof,
ignores crow and human glare alike, aloof
and barefoot. How those tiles must burn
as she waits till noon, without move or turn.

A foot steps out of the sari,
like a cautious animal, wary.
Her back arches, her head and arms
describe half-moons, her fingers charms.

Under the hot, hot sun she maintains
a slow, slow dance that contains
continents and constellations within
its moves, and dreams in its skin.

The sweat pours down with each beat
and gathers in pools at her feet,
the only water for acres around,
and deep deep, her toes already drowned.

She's a needle piercing the sky,
and now if you look hard and try
and squint, you imagine you see a place
or two darkening in the sky's blue face.

Like wolves on hunt, cloud
after cloud gathers, their proud,
growling thunder rolls and bounces
off concrete and eardrum and announces

the rain.

And the rain that pours
is like
forgiveness,
like a benediction.
The earth explodes with fragrance
and small children and old men
run outdoors to
be engulfed, to be swept away.
And it rains and it rains,
and the sound of the rain
fills the ear, banishes away every
small meanness, every fretful
concern over tomorrow.
And it rains like it will never stop.

And the woman on the roof
kneels on the tiles,
her body both pushed down
and held upright by the rain.
And during an especially heavy
cloudburst,
children from neighbouring buildings
all swear she melted away
into the rain.

And after the rain is done,
no one remembers her, not even one.
In fact the Parmars in number 16,
would swear their flat is the last,
that there never was a woman or a flat
number 17.

Offering

The first offerings to the rains
are always from the trees.
Trembling and shivering in the wind,
they bow their bodies, drunk on showers.

After them, the world changes itself
into a series of small pools and rivers
afloat on the pitted brown bodies of roads
tossed across each other like fallen tree trunks.

Red buses roar across them ceaselessly
like healthy animals, careless of
lesser creatures and indifferent
to the clean shine of their own hides.

And from me also the rain plucks
an offering like a jealous goddess.
At first, she touches my brow and lips
with liquid softness to remind me.

Then she rakes her cold fingernails
down my chest, across my back,
paints my skin with shivers and
waters my eyes with reproachful tears.

She plays a silent music through
the narrow flutes of my veins and arteries.
My body thrums to the silent music—
alveoli puff like small balloons.

A few explode like raindrops and
at the end of a coughing fit, I produce
two red spots on a white handkerchief,
and the music is allowed to subside.

My body is bowed like a tree, held up
by the weak branches of my arms.
The first offerings to the rains
are always from the trees.

Coming and Going

Seasons

Before, your thin wick burnt
unnoticed, aflame in summer heat.
Now stumble, stumble in the cold rain
dissolving your melted misshapen feet.

Duck

Out from the mouth
of an inter-city bus, I
emerge gingerly from the mist
of early morning sleepiness.

A small forgettable stop,
like so many others, where always
the same cup of tea bubbles up
as if from a shared reservoir.

On a grassy patch a duck
squats half-asleep, its neck
turned backwards, bill buried
in the feathers of its back.

As the bus leaves, it stirs briefly,
tastes the morning air, full of the
danger of lonely departure, and sinks
gratefully back into soft feathery sleep.

Mukteshwar

You had the word and
the name of the place,
while I was a careless
passenger wandering with you
up those brown and green
roads, past lakes as still
as emerald pores in the
mountain side, and when
we found a temple that
had not been drunk dry
by pilgrims you did not
hesitate, but walked in and
around it with an unfaltering
step while I bent at first
and then bumped my head
on the roof of the world.

As we drove back I
remember we bought apples
whose sourness would remain
untasted in a mad rush for
luggage and that as we passed
the last lake, my toes,
safely socked and shoed away,
strained a little as if they
realized that they had mistaken
the deep warmth of green water
for a cold they would never
have been able to bear.

Mango Fudge

Part I—Recipe

Holidays
are made of this—
a basin of warm weather,
filled with a generous helping
of days as easy as
a lazy

river on a leash,
friendly chatter like cold beer
down a throat dry with
shouting at four walls,
moments

of drunk laughter
silly humour, not pieced out
in chance bites but spread
smooth and deep delicious.
The sun

a generous mango dollop
on a plate of sky.
A day you reach into
a bag of sweets with
no fear of finding
empty wrappers.

Part II—Digestion

Confessions after the second
evening drink are the easiest
to forget and swallow with
the next.

It's the mid-afternoon
story of a child's death
that makes you think of
the screams

that have no walls
to bounce off here, perhaps
they collect as those black
river-shore rocks

hidden under deep skirts
of water in some weather,
in others lying naked, bawling
to the sun.

Part III—Fudged

The woods are silent
when they creep up on you.
The woods are silent and still.
You ride an empty road
comfortably through a country
of burnt grass and rock,
until

they're on you in
row after row, still and bare.
Regiment after regiment they drill
past—a sepia evening parade
coming at you in thin
slices

of time, as if
this road dipped in and out
of sleep as it dices
talk into slow spaced words,
scattering breadcrumbs of sound,
smelling

of sweet witch cake
that stains your hand yellow
as you try to ring the bell
on this door of perception
that remains closed for yet
another spell.

Maps

When I was seven my parents
had their bedroom walls painted
a shade best described as
indifferent cream.

But in a few months seepage
and an occasional tennis ball,
had caused pieces to flake
and break off.

And I saw it then—
my first map, a filthy
cream sea and islands of
exposed green paint.

I named those islands and
continents of green, and then
discarded those names as unworthy,
and simply watched

as they grew and aged
at a glacial pace, always
changing and always the same,
and undeniably real.

I saw them again two
decades later in a cheap
hotel room, dull yellow bulbs
lighting up the

crumbling paint on a blank
wall in just the right
way, my seas and continents
returned to me.

Once again changed and once
again staying just the same.
My fingers traced powdery plaster,
confirming sharp edges

of gulfs and straits and
unnamed bays, trying to retain
the memory of what would be lost
the next day.

And now, fifty years old
with a heart that's giving
up on me, I've found
the third map.

I found it one morning,
naked in front of a bathroom
mirror, my scars and moles
and lines and

birthmarks all revealed to me
as a pattern, my map
that I've been carrying
with me all along.

All the islands and plains
and the mountains and lakes
are there, with something new
added to the map.

A tilted cross of scar tissue
over my heart is what I
now realize I've always needed,
always waited for.

Every map is a journey,
and every journey always needs
a starting point, a place
to begin, and as always,
X marks the spot.

Closed Rooms

Moonlight

The air tonight is as clear
as a pool of water.
So many things have gathered
shape tonight, hard and unforgiving.

They no longer murmur to me
in disjointed geometries.
Tonight they lie orderly,
like letters on a page.

Tonight, even the cement road
seems smooth, without the stubble
of small stones and potholes,
an unblemished grey sheet.

I might lay my smooth cheek
against it, the short swim
of air between here and there
is invitingly cool to my skin.

It is easy to imagine—
my body soft in sleep under
a streetlamp whose light
congeals under my fingertips.

Time flutters for a moment,
like a page from a book,
and then lies still and cool
undisturbed by my breath.

Reborn

I was reborn on a
white-tiled bathroom floor,
baptized in phenyl fumes,
my eyes learning their first
colours in a sea of
pornographically repeated
gleaming whites.

I learned to walk, toes
tickled by the dust
settled onto hallway
carpets, motes whispering
to me the real name
of each identical door,
signposts for the arbitrary.

I died several times.
Once,
on a slow walk to the end
of a corridor, my skin
burning away in
thick white copper smoke,
the whole of my body
sublimating and then
congealing in thick
droplets on the walls and ceiling.

Another time,
I stepped into a lift.
Its doors closed behind
me with a soft thump.
And inside, no buttons,
no floors, no alarms, no escapes
no movement.
A smooth metal tomb,
disturbed only by
my slowly shrinking breath.

Once,
I lived a century of seconds,
maybe more,
each second split into a
thousand drops of oil,
each of which I carried
dangling from the edge of an
aching finger tip
down a score of granite steps
to the mouth of a generator
that sucked at it with metal teeth
and breath that stank of blood.

And once,
I walked into a room
full of people talking like stars,
their mouths dribbling sunlight,
their hands moving through the air
like meteors, and when they
turned towards me, their stares
burnt my frail body
to a fine ash, leaving
behind only my spectacle-
protected eyes to measure
the million-step distance
between us, and the
tip of a finger resting
on the door, and closing it
now, feeling it only
keyhole wide. This
was the quickest
of all the times I died.

Equations for a Wooden Door

Let's start with the simplest one:
two dimensions.

height x width = area

There's only so much you can let in
at one time, or so you imagine.
You raise your roof, time after time,
and each time bend lower, when you
need to step out into the sun.

Three dimensions now.

height x width x depth = volume

You believe you can look at
the toe of a thing before the foot
is in, gauge, understand and judge it
before it is real, but this assumes
that everything knocks before entering.

And now a harder one.

$\pi r^2/4$ = the floor area covered by an opening door

There's always some furniture
you need to move out of the way,
padlocks to open, eyeholes to check,
and always that temptation to be avoided—
escaping through an open window.

When It Starts

The moment you hear
the breath of fire
out of someone's mouth
on the phone line
on the flickering face
of an e-mail.

The moment when you
throw on all the lights
trying to sweep away
the lizard shadows
curling all too fast
in the corners.

When you no longer
buy tickets
last moment,
when you check the
tyres even though
you're not driving.

When you can no more
walk through doors
and padlocked gates
and officious faces
like they're not there,
because now, they are.

The City

The Unguarded Street

I walk down an empty street, unguarded
when a voice behind me calls out and says,
'Madarchod.'
Just like that.
Like a knife thrown in the dark.
Three syllables that say—
turn around,
turn around and show your face.
Your bearded chin,
your ash-smeared forehead.
Drop your pants, drop
your self-assurance,
so I can hate you.
Tell me, my prisoner
your name—your full name,
that is also your social rank
and the serial number
of your caste.

And now, what?
What do I do?
With this gaali in a galli
that is sure to be followed
by its sister phrase
'Behenchod'.
Do I pick up a fist
to throw at him or turn
as I have before
yet another cheek?
The remains of the earth
after all, will be inherited
by the meek.

And what if I use words
love words—father
brother
and mother and father
and brother and sister.
What if I say love
over and over again
like water eroding stone
but also like
empty buckets of air
on a fire?

What if I do this or something else?
Sticks and stones and broken bones.
What if I die nameless
on an unguarded street?

The City When It Sleeps

Walking a railway bridge
at night, note the moment
for which yours is the only
footstep in hearing, that's when
you can feel it blink.

Sometimes there is a pattern,
in the on-off blink of
streetlamps, and the breeze
down the street stinks of
the breath of a hungry animal.

The city dreams invisibly.
Two a.m. drunks stumble upon
the feral offspring of streets
hunting with brick and glass
baiting their drainpipe traps
with the soft music of safety.

There are streets, sometimes
a strip of dambar and dust
between high rises and slums,
sometimes concrete between identical
slabs of a housing colony.

The people in each building
will come out on the road,
unstumbling in its dark silence,
and lie down to sleep
on the dirt, breaths mingling.

They will lie undisturbed
for a few dark hours, then
go back to slotted consciousness
brushing aside dirt in their hair,
changing rain-damp clothing, careless
in the morning of their unconcern.

Stopping at All Stations

It starts early, the first train of the day.
It has to, to account for the delay
in all the others.
Get in. Get in.
Run hard. Run hard.

Five minutes between off-hours and rush.
Two trains between empty seats and the crush.
In between there's chai.
Come in. Come in.
Look out. Look out.

Exercise—squeeze stomach in and arch back,
plant left foot flat, right one in the crack
in the tangle of chappals.
Squeeze in. Squeeze in.
Squeeze out. Squeeze out.

There's stretches of platform, open to the sky.
You looked up once, imagined you could fly,
then rushed
to miss your bus.
Get off. Get off.
Work hard. Work hard.

Meals, Large and Small

Set Dosa

It comes in five pieces. A pieced-out mash of yellow potatoes wrapped in five pieces of crisp, brown dosa cloth. With impeccable accuracy, the waiter puts down the plate exactly in-between the two of us. The sambhar is like nectar. I can tell that even before I taste it, as I watch you swallow a spoon of it and see its colour spreading on your cheeks. We never talk while we eat. At least, not with words. You won't speak even to disapprove of the way I dump the sambhar and chutney on my piece of dosa before swallowing it, treating red-orange nectar and green ambrosia like they were just two flavours of ketchup. I still haven't absorbed the habit of having them separately with a spoon, like you do. You only speak when we get to the fifth piece. You say in mock pleading, 'But I'm hungry.' And I have to laugh, and surrender spoon and fork.

A light drizzle has started outside the restaurant. We have two cups of coffee while we wait for it to stop. We blow the cool air of nostalgia over warm reminisces and sip carefully of the not-yet-ordered future. We avoid talking about the present. As if it were something that needs to be held just right—like these stainless steel coffee cups, filled to the brim, held just at the top, too loose and it spills over you, too tight and you burn yourself.

It's still raining, even after we pay the bill and walk out. But for once, you don't mind being led out into a warm drizzle. And I don't mind either. It's been years since I walked you home in the rain.

Frying Fish

Contrary to what they've told you,
these days there are fewer and fewer
fish in the sea.

Hard to find, harder to find
fresh. You can order them online,
but pictures are useless.

When you pick a slice of fish,
you want to look at it as
it looks at you.

Strong-boned surmai that are simple
and uncomplicated, pretty pomfrets that
you'll score with a knife for
what you say is their own good.
Whole bombils weighted down to
remove water, flattened out so
that you can ask them later
why they're so dry.

Every slice deserves love and patience.
Balance the mirchi powder and the salt,
water and common sense, and remember haldi—
a pinch of disinfectant is not
a lack of trust.

Over the years you've come to terms
with the fact that the oil
will always be tepid or too hot.
The only thing you're careful about
is not to splash.

Also, there will always be burns.
The ones above your wrist are
easy to hide, you're always careful
to keep your face away if
you can help it.

So even in this dried-out summer
heat, you look and you look,
fishing without hooks, lures or tricks.
You know nothing tastes quite like
a slice of fish, and nothing quite like
one that is shared.

Lunch with the Aztecs

We sit down to eat
in pleasing familiarity—
tomatoes,
beans,
the perfume of flowers,
freshly picked.
The mother smiles at me
with folded hands.
'In the bathroom,'
she says,
'father's in the bathroom,
shaving.'
I imagine him.
The last smooth scrape
complete,
he considers the blade
and why not?
An offering,
a minute sacrifice,
a slice of skin
for family health,
a promotion,
kinder neighbours.

I wonder,
if I listen close
under the sound
of my breath,
what will it sound like?
Knife
splitting skin like butter
or the wicked, wicked
sawing through
of tough leather,
and will it boil over
like thin red lava
or splatter, splatter rush
out like a river,
subterranean once,
now liberated.

And then he will sit
with us,
his fresh wounds glowing
with the pride
of paternal self-sacrifice.

And the snake will dance
before me,
its thick green body
swelling
with its sap of life,
adorned with feathers,
bright, bright feathers.

Atop the dizzying heights
of a decaying pyramid
I will squint
uncertainly
into a valley of bones
sharpened to daggers
and count which ones
I arrange for my enemies
and, which ones
are arranged for me.

Fur and Wing

The Black Dog's Ghost

Most times it's the smell
of him that wakes me,
a brush of fur on the arm
startles me awake, heart pounding.

Sometimes I come home
to see him sitting there,
holding the living room prisoner,
in his rough pawed silence.

I know what you think,
but I didn't kill him.
I merely watched him die,
a bleeding hit-and-run accident.

Sometimes, I think he's just
a companion or a guide,
for here or later, and sometimes
a hungry waiting beast.

The Other Butterfly That Stamped

A man, looking out a window spies
two butterflies in a tree—
a male outside, while a female lies

emerging from her cocoon, still not free.
The male over eager to mate,
tears at the cocoon impatiently.

The man makes jokes at their fate—
Can't emerge now, my hair's not dry,
reservations at seven, we'll be late.

He watches the male try after try,
and then sees him fly away
into a lonely piece of sky.

The man imagines him making his way
in through window onto instrument panel,
a green-yellow stone in a garden of grey,

floating and landing in a careless channel
of buttons, activating sequence pins
that launch missiles whose metallic enamel

like the teeth of fire-bearded djinns
open up to swallow a city complete
in a single giant mushroom, that spins

out a gift of radiational heat
that warms the female butterfly,
now emerged and in all conceit

fluttering impatiently, wondering why
her mate wandered off and whether
the suddenly darkening sky

is another case of butterfly weather.

A Lament on Sparrows

The wind strolls in from the West
on smog-coloured slippers.
It removes them respectfully,
before stepping into AC ducts.

Inside buildings there is talk,
lunch-break, coffee-break laments.
The city is emptying of birds—
avian extinction, biscuits and elaichi tea.

There used to be so many sparrows,
parliaments of them on every other street.
Now they've all been swept away,
like so many discarded brown leaves.

The city is overrun with crows.
They perch on terrace ledges,
dark eyes glinting like keys
hung on a jailer's belt.

And overrun with pigeons,
stumbling clumsily over each other,
falling into view like pairs
of plump, startled teenagers

The city is growing into a museum
of itself, and yesterday's commonplace
is spun into today's myth.
Fancy gathers fact into its wings.

A round-faced man talks of parrots.
He might suddenly explode into a flock
of them, his skin opening like a bag,
releasing a sea of green feathers.

A small woman talks excitedly
of mynahs, her waving arms,
conducting in a line of black and yellow
birds, disorderly like impatient taxi-cabs.

Blue feathers are pushing through my skin.
I muse on the name of the creature
soon to push out from me onto
the wind moving West into the sun.

Words on Words

The Sand Libraries of Timbuktu

What does a book that's been
silent for seven hundred years
say when you open it?

Does it mutter half-sentences
in crumbling dusty dialects?
Or do the words burst out
of the page inexplicably like
a spring rising out of desert sand?

Perhaps the books are more ordinary,
and like their curators
firework-bereft and bald.
Tracts political, historical,
astronomical, and all in verse.
Enlightening, undramatic, practical,
their ancient authors
unencumbered by the West.

How often has a book that's been
passed from generation to generation
been read out loud?

Enough trickling out perhaps
to stain shores more familiar now.
A Sufi tale or two in Andersen's
with clothing heavier for the Danish cold.
The silvery glint of a medical
treatise in Crusoe's empty island.

Which of these thousands of books,
which of these millions of pages
soon to be gathered up by academic
hordes, by armies of vain collectors,
will be left to the careless wayfarer
to be found as unexpected oases?

Perhaps a thin sheaf of love poems,
like the claws of a meaty beast
cast off as offal, but still the shape
of those that still mark our flesh
as we stumble blindly in the desert
in the slow search for the Caravan.

Listen

Listen,
tea rhymes with gold,
or better still with
sunlight breaking through
the trees,

the coldness of stone
with the first touch
of a still pool
of water.

There's music
in sea-waves breaking
at dawn,

in watching a man walk,
watching a woman walk,
or a child run
across a street.

I could paint you
a whole story
using only

the peach-soft touch
of a first kiss

the hunger of
the endless empty hours
of midnight

the roll of
cool water down
a parched throat

the touch and
embrace of skin
warm as honey

and with the burning
lonely shame
of tears.

Listen,
when I speak,
even in my silence.

The best poems
are written in silence,
to the rhythm
of a beating heart.

This Poem

This poem will start simple
and speak straight to you
because you wrote it yourself,
but
you will forget this poem
as soon as you've heard it.

This is the poem you
tried to write at sixteen
and would have at thirty,
if not busy buying a living.

This poem will change nothing.
This poem was written in Bombay.
This poem is a road
you can either walk down
or rename.

This poem has seen death,
in fatal railway-track crossings
and exploded second-class carriages,
blood on riot-born swords
and from everyday
mosquito bites of indifference.

This poem has cried itself to flooding,
drowned in its own tears,
and still lived to complain
about the city's lack of drainage.

This poem is sunlight
and life-giving rain. It
rises up and shakes its
filth-covered fist at the sun
laughing at its own bruises.

This poem is dead. It
wrote itself on the back of
an unencashed compensation cheque
passed from father to son.

This poem is ordinary, that's
why it is beautiful.
This poem is breath-sweet
smog-coloured concrete-scented
breath, the scent thrown off
by huge metal animals
in a steel and brick forest.

This poem would be ordinary
if it were beautiful
with burgundy-dyed similes
and streaky-blond allusions,
but this poem is bald.
It uses none of its
own words, instead it uses
ten-rupee roadside words
stuffed in paos, with onions
and two types of chutney.

This poem is washed over
in the surf of a thousand
other poems whose sentences
clamber over it like children
reaching for a view of the tamasha
and yet its shoulders stay strong.

This poem will win no awards.
This poem is unoriginal.
This poem comes without intervals
or toilet breaks, this poem
would be longer if the neighbours
didn't play-their-music-so-fucking-loud.

This poem is a thief.
It sips your sweetest dreams,
gorges on your laughter,
wins your children's adoration,
fucks your wife, your husband
and leaves you to navigate
those empty afternoon hours alone.

This poem is always simple
and speaks straight to you
but
you always forget this poem
as soon as you've heard it
because you write it yourself.

Acknowledgements

Poems are creatures that can be hard to trap in the easiest of times. I am thankful to the many people who've helped me snare them along the way, and also to the people who've helped me keep them alive, healthy and presentable.

Jhumur Ghosh for support, encouragement and the kindling of that rare spark of self-belief.

Sudarshan Purohit for being an unflagging and supportive first reader, and for teaching me the value of finishing every piece.

Ranjit Hoskote, Jerry Pinto and Arundhathi Subramaniam for opportunity and their always warm support and encouragement.

The Jehangir Sabavala Foundation and the team at Speaking Tiger for belief and opportunity.

My family, with whom words first began for me and without whom I'd have written very little.

Peter Griffin and Manisha Lakhe of Caferati. The earliest of these poems were ones I first read out at Caferati read-meets.

And finally to all those who read and listened. These poems only live when you allow them to walk amongst you.

ACKNOWLEDGEMENTS

[illegible]